My Home Workbook

My Home Workbook

**The essential
home owner's record-keeper**
—— *for* ——
Costs, repairs,
finance details, improvements,
renovations, monthly to-do lists,
chores, phone numbers,
—— *and more* ——

by Mimi Tribble

**Sterling Publishing Co., Inc.
New York**

Library of Congress Cataloging-in-Publication Data Available

2 3 4 5 6 7 8 9 10

Published by Sterling Publishing Co., Inc.
387 Park Avenue South, New York, NY 10016
© 2004 by Sterling Publishing Co., Inc.
Distributed in Canada by Sterling Publishing
c/o Canadian Manda Group, 165 Dufferin Street,
Toronto, Ontario, Canada M6K 3H6
Distributed in Great Britain by GMC Distribution Services,
Castle Place, 166 High Street, Lewes, East Sussex, England BN7 1XU
Distributed in Australia by Capricorn Link (Australia) Pty. Ltd.
P.O. Box 704, Windsor, NSW 2756, Australia

Designed by Liz Trovato
Printed in China
All rights reserved

Sterling ISBN-13: 978-1-4027-1263-0
ISBN-10: 1-4027-1263-4

For information about custom editions, special sales, premium and
corporate purchases, please contact Sterling Special Sales
Department at 800-805-5489 or specialsales@sterlingpub.com.

*If lost, please
return to:*

Name:

Address:

Phone:

Contents

Important Contacts

Service	Name	Phone
Air Conditioner Repair		
Carpenter		
Carpet Cleaner		
Cleaning Service		
Drapery Cleaner		
Electrician		
Exterminator		
General Handyman		
Heating Repair		
Lawn Service		
Home Insurance		
Painter		
Paperer		
Plumber		
Roof Repair		
Sewer/Cesspool/ Septic System		
Other		

Notes

Second Mortgage Company

Loan No.   Phone

Date

Balance of Principal on Original

Mortgage Information

Purchase Price   Price Asked

Down Payment

Appraised Value

Mortgage Amount

Location of Abstract

Mortgage Type *(FHA, VA, Conventional, etc.)*

Interest Rate *(beginning, if adjustable*)*

Terms *(30 yr. fixed, adjustable,* etc.)*

Points *(no. & $ amount)*

Realtor's Commission *(% & $)*

Closing Date

Other Closing Costs

*Adjustable Rate Mortgage (ARM) Information

Rate	Date of Change	Principal Remaining	Monthly P & I

Adjustment Interval

Index   Margin

Interest Rate Caps *(yearly, lifetime, etc.)*

Monthly Payment Cap

Graduated Payments

Negative Amortization *(y/n & limit)*

"Introductory" Rate

Assumability   Convertibility

Prepayment Privilege

Points *(including origination fee)*

Other

Insurance Information

Title Insurance Information

Title Binders No.

Home Owner's Insurance Company

Agent's Name   Office Phone

Cell Phone   Policy No.

Expiration Date *(Month & Day)*

Taxes and the Sale of Your Home

The information presented in this section is to help you plan for the sale of your home along the way, but is not a substitute for a dialog with a well-versed attorney or accountant when you are ready to sell.

A capital gain is an increase in the value of a capital asset, in this case real estate, higher than the purchase price. Relevant to the sale of your home, the gain is realized when the asset is sold and must be claimed on income taxes. Tax breaks, however, are granted on assets held longer than 18 months and for homesteads or primary residences.

To reduce your capital gains tax, you can increase your tax basis by documenting everything that increases the initial tax base, or the purchase price of the home. The tax basis can be calculated on costs related to the purchase of your home such as attorney and escrow fees, title costs, and loan placement charges and also on improvements to the home, including additional rooms, heating system, land improvements, and a new roof.

Thorough documentation of any improvement or increase to the tax basis, however, is essential to lower your capital gains tax. Hence, it is very important to keep all receipts and documents relevant to the tax basis of your home. *The Home Workbook* and the following Tax Worksheet centralize information pertinent to the improvement of your home, such as key dates, contacts, costs, and notes concerning the purchase of your home.

While improvements add to the value of your home, repairs do not. Repairs include things done to keep your home operating daily such as repainting, fixing cracks, and replacing anything. Although repairs are not tax deductible, it is still important to keep track of them to save time and money in the future.

Tax Worksheet

	Amount
Original Cost of Home	
Add Closing Costs:	
Legal Fees	
Appraisal Fee	
Commission Fee to Broker	
Escrow Fee	
Title Cost	
State Deed Taxes and Filing Fees	
Loan Placement Fees (e.g. Points)	
Other	

Notes

Add Remodeling and Renovations Made:

Date	Description	Amount

Add Improvements Made:

Date	Description	Amount

Important Personal Papers

List of what they are, where they are kept, and the people associated with them. For example, wills, various insurance policies and the appropriate attorneys and agents.

 Interior

Living Room

Floor Covering

Floor Measurements

Widest part of room from middle of doorway

Longest part of room from middle of doorway

Type of Floor

Purchased from   Date

Brand & Patterns

Color & No.   Warranty Period

Type of Backing   Pad Type

Cost/Unit $ No. of Units   Total $

Installed by   Date   Cost

Cleaned/Refinished by

Date 1   Cost

Date 2   Cost

Date 3   Cost

Ceiling Covering

Type of Covering

Purchased from   Date

Brand & Pattern

Color & No.   Warranty Period

Applied with

Cost/Unit $ No. of Units   Total $

Installed by   Date   Cost

Window Covering

Window 1

Measurements

Height	Width
Top of Window to Floor	Trim Width

Type of Covering

Purchased from	Cost	Date

Measurements of Window Covering

Material & Cleaning Instructions		
Cleaned by	Cost	Date
Cleaned by	Cost	Date

Window 2

Measurements

Height	Width
Top of Window to Floor	Trim Width

Type of Covering

Purchased from	Cost	Date

Measurements of Window Covering

Material & Cleaning Instructions		
Cleaned by	Cost	Date
Cleaned by	Cost	Date

Window 3

Measurements

Height	Width
Top of Window to Floor	Trim Width

Type of Covering

Purchased from   Cost   Date

Measurements of Window Covering

Material & Cleaning Instructions

Cleaned by   Cost   Date

Cleaned by   Cost   Date

Wall Covering

Wall Measurements

North   South   East   West

Use "2nd Type of Covering" for woodwork or paneling. It has a "Refinished by" section.

1st Type of Covering

Purchased from   Date

Brand & Pattern

Color & No.   Warranty Period

Cost/Unit $ No. of Units   Total $

Installed by   Date   Cost

2nd Type of Covering

Purchased from   Date

Brand & Pattern

Color & No.   Warranty Period

Cost/Unit $ No. of Units   Total $

Installed by   Date   Cost

Refinished by   Date   Cost

Notes

Doors/Trim

Purchased from	Date
Brand & Style	Material
Stain/Paint Color & No.	Finished with
Installed by	Total Cost
Refinished by	Refinished with
Date	Cost
Hardware Description	
Purchased from	Date
Cost/Unit $	No. of Units	Total $

Furniture/Fixtures

Item	Purchased from	Date	Cost	Warranty

Dining Room

Floor Covering

Floor Measurements

Widest part of room from middle of doorway

Longest part of room from middle of doorway

Type of Floor

Purchased from   Date

Brand & Patterns

Color & No.   Warranty Period

Type of Backing   Pad Type

Cost/Unit $ No. of Units   Total $

Installed by   Date   Cost

Cleaned/Refinished by

Date 1   Cost

Date 2   Cost

Date 3   Cost

Ceiling Covering

Type of Covering

Purchased from   Date

Brand & Pattern

Color & No.   Warranty Period

Applied with

Cost/Unit $ No. of Units   Total $

Installed by   Date   Cost

Window Covering

Window 1

Measurements

Height _____ Width _____

Top of Window to Floor _____ Trim Width _____

Type of Covering

Purchased from _____ Cost _____ Date _____

Measurements of Window Covering

Material & Cleaning Instructions _____

Cleaned by _____ Cost _____ Date _____

Cleaned by _____ Cost _____ Date _____

Window 2

Measurements

Height _____ Width _____

Top of Window to Floor _____ Trim Width _____

Type of Covering

Purchased from _____ Cost _____ Date _____

Measurements of Window Covering

Material & Cleaning Instructions _____

Cleaned by _____ Cost _____ Date _____

Cleaned by _____ Cost _____ Date _____

Window 3

Measurements

Height _____ Width _____

Top of Window to Floor _____ Trim Width _____

Type of Covering

Purchased from   Cost   Date

Measurements of Window Covering

Material & Cleaning Instructions

Cleaned by   Cost   Date

Cleaned by   Cost   Date

Wall Covering

Wall Measurements

North   South   East   West

Use "2nd Type of Covering" for woodwork or paneling. It has a "Refinished by" section.

1st Type of Covering

Purchased from   Date

Brand & Pattern

Color & No.   Warranty Period

Cost/Unit $ No. of Units   Total $

Installed by   Date   Cost

2nd Type of Covering

Purchased from   Date

Brand & Pattern

Color & No.   Warranty Period

Cost/Unit $ No. of Units   Total $

Installed by   Date   Cost

Refinished by   Date   Cost

Doors/Trim

Purchased from	Date
Brand & Style	Material
Stain/Paint Color & No.	Finished with
Installed by	Total Cost
Refinished by	Refinished with
Date	Cost
Hardware Description	
Purchased from	Date
Cost/Unit $ No. of Units	Total $

Furniture/Fixtures

Item	Purchased from	Date	Cost	Warranty

Kitchen

Floor Covering

Floor Measurements

Widest part of room from middle of doorway

Longest part of room from middle of doorway

Type of Floor

Purchased from   Date

Brand & Patterns

Color & No.   Warranty Period

Type of Backing   Pad Type

Cost/Unit $ No. of Units   Total $

Installed by   Date   Cost

Cleaned/Refinished by

Date 1   Cost

Date 2   Cost

Date 3   Cost

Ceiling Covering

Type of Covering

Purchased from   Date

Brand & Pattern

Color & No.   Warranty Period

Applied with

Cost/Unit $ No. of Units   Total $

Installed by   Date   Cost

Window Covering

Window 1

Measurements

Height	Width	
Top of Window to Floor	Trim Width	

Type of Covering

Purchased from	Cost	Date

Measurements of Window Covering

Material & Cleaning Instructions		
Cleaned by	Cost	Date
Cleaned by	Cost	Date

Window 2

Measurements

Height	Width	
Top of Window to Floor	Trim Width	

Type of Covering

Purchased from	Cost	Date

Measurements of Window Covering

Material & Cleaning Instructions		
Cleaned by	Cost	Date
Cleaned by	Cost	Date

Window 3

Measurements

Height	Width	
Top of Window to Floor	Trim Width	

Type of Covering

Purchased from   Cost   Date

Measurements of Window Covering

Material & Cleaning Instructions

Cleaned by   Cost   Date

Cleaned by   Cost   Date

Wall Covering

Wall Measurements

North   South   East   West

Use "2nd Type of Covering" for woodwork or paneling. It has a "Refinished by" section.

1st Type of Covering

Purchased from   Date

Brand & Pattern

Color & No.   Warranty Period

Cost/Unit $ No. of Units   Total $

Installed by   Date   Cost

2nd Type of Covering

Purchased from   Date

Brand & Pattern

Color & No.   Warranty Period

Cost/Unit $ No. of Units   Total $

Installed by   Date   Cost

Refinished by   Date   Cost

Notes

Cabinets

Purchased from   Date

Brand & Style

Material

Stain/Paint Color & No.   Finished with

Countertop Material

Brand & Pattern

Color & No.   Installed by

Refinished by   Total Cost

Refinished with   Date   Cost

Hardware Description

Purchased from   Date

Cost/Unit $ No. of Units   Total $

Doors/Trim

Purchased from   Date

Brand & Style   Material

Stain/Paint Color & No.   Finished with

Installed by   Total Cost

Refinished by   Refinished with

Date   Cost

Hardware Description

Purchased from   Date

Cost/Unit $ No. of Units   Total $

Major Appliances

Type

Manufacturer   Model/Lot No.   Serial No.

Purchased from   Cost   Date

Authorized Service Center

Warranty Period   Maintenance/Service

Type

Manufacturer   Model/Lot No.   Serial No.

Purchased from   Cost   Date

Authorized Service Center

Warranty Period   Maintenance/Service

Type

Manufacturer   Model/Lot No.   Serial No.

Purchased from   Cost   Date

Authorized Service Center

Warranty Period   Maintenance/Service

Type

Manufacturer   Model/Lot No.   Serial No.

Purchased from   Cost   Date

Authorized Service Center

Warranty Period   Maintenance/Service

Type

Manufacturer   Model/Lot No.   Serial No.

Purchased from   Cost   Date

Authorized Service Center

Warranty Period   Maintenance/Service

Type

Manufacturer   Model/Lot No.   Serial No.

Purchased from   Cost   Date

Authorized Service Center

Warranty Period   Maintenance/Service

Furniture/Fixtures/Small Appliances

Item	Purchased from	Date	Cost	Warranty

Bedroom Number 1

Floor Covering

Floor Measurements

Widest part of room from middle of doorway

Longest part of room from middle of doorway

Type of Floor

Purchased from   Date

Brand & Patterns

Color & No.   Warranty Period

Type of Backing   Pad Type

Cost/Unit $ No. of Units   Total $

Installed by   Date   Cost

Cleaned/Refinished by

Date 1   Cost

Date 2   Cost

Date 3   Cost

Ceiling Covering

Type of Covering

Purchased from   Date

Brand & Pattern

Color & No.   Warranty Period

Applied with

Cost/Unit $ No. of Units   Total $

Installed by   Date   Cost

Window Covering

Window 1

Measurements

Height	Width
Top of Window to Floor	Trim Width

Type of Covering

Purchased from	Cost	Date

Measurements of Window Covering

Material & Cleaning Instructions

Cleaned by	Cost	Date
Cleaned by	Cost	Date

Window 2

Measurements

Height	Width
Top of Window to Floor	Trim Width

Type of Covering

Purchased from	Cost	Date

Measurements of Window Covering

Material & Cleaning Instructions

Cleaned by	Cost	Date
Cleaned by	Cost	Date

Window 3

Measurements

Height	Width
Top of Window to Floor	Trim Width

Type of Covering

Purchased from   Cost   Date

Measurements of Window Covering

Material & Cleaning Instructions

Cleaned by   Cost   Date

Cleaned by   Cost   Date

Wall Covering

Wall Measurements

North   South   East   West

Use "2nd Type of Covering" for woodwork or paneling. It has a "Refinished by" section.

1st Type of Covering

Purchased from   Date

Brand & Pattern

Color & No.   Warranty Period

Cost/Unit $ No. of Units   Total $

Installed by   Date   Cost

2nd Type of Covering

Purchased from   Date

Brand & Pattern

Color & No.   Warranty Period

Cost/Unit $ No. of Units   Total $

Installed by   Date   Cost

Refinished by   Date   Cost

Doors/Trim

Purchased from	Date
Brand & Style	Material
Stain/Paint Color & No.	Finished with
Installed by	Total Cost
Refinished by	Refinished with
Date	Cost
Hardware Description	
Purchased from	Date
Cost/Unit $ No. of Units	Total $

Furniture/Fixtures

Item	Purchased from	Date	Cost	Warranty

Bedroom Number 2

Floor Covering

Floor Measurements

Widest part of room from middle of doorway

Longest part of room from middle of doorway

Type of Floor

Purchased from   Date

Brand & Patterns

Color & No.   Warranty Period

Type of Backing   Pad Type

Cost/Unit $ No. of Units   Total $

Installed by   Date   Cost

Cleaned/Refinished by

Date 1   Cost

Date 2   Cost

Date 3   Cost

Ceiling Covering

Type of Covering

Purchased from   Date

Brand & Pattern

Color & No.   Warranty Period

Applied with

Cost/Unit $ No. of Units   Total $

Installed by   Date   Cost

Window Covering

Window 1

Measurements

Height _____ Width _____

Top of Window to Floor _____ Trim Width _____

Type of Covering

Purchased from _____ Cost _____ Date _____

Measurements of Window Covering

Material & Cleaning Instructions _____

Cleaned by _____ Cost _____ Date _____

Cleaned by _____ Cost _____ Date _____

Window 2

Measurements

Height _____ Width _____

Top of Window to Floor _____ Trim Width _____

Type of Covering

Purchased from _____ Cost _____ Date _____

Measurements of Window Covering

Material & Cleaning Instructions _____

Cleaned by _____ Cost _____ Date _____

Cleaned by _____ Cost _____ Date _____

Window 3

Measurements

Height _____ Width _____

Top of Window to Floor _____ Trim Width _____

Type of Covering

Purchased from   Cost   Date

Measurements of Window Covering

Material & Cleaning Instructions

Cleaned by   Cost   Date

Cleaned by   Cost   Date

Wall Covering

Wall Measurements

North   South   East   West

Use "2nd Type of Covering" for woodwork or paneling. It has a "Refinished by" section.

1st Type of Covering

Purchased from   Date

Brand & Pattern

Color & No.   Warranty Period

Cost/Unit $ No. of Units   Total $

Installed by   Date   Cost

2nd Type of Covering

Purchased from   Date

Brand & Pattern

Color & No.   Warranty Period

Cost/Unit $ No. of Units   Total $

Installed by   Date   Cost

Refinished by   Date   Cost

Doors/Trim

Purchased from   Date

Brand & Style   Material

Stain/Paint Color & No.   Finished with

Installed by   Total Cost

Refinished by   Refinished with

Date   Cost

Hardware Description

Purchased from   Date

Cost/Unit $ No. of Units   Total $

Furniture/Fixtures

Item	Purchased from	Date	Cost	Warranty

Bedroom Number 3

Floor Covering

Floor Measurements

Widest part of room from middle of doorway

Longest part of room from middle of doorway

Type of Floor

Purchased from Date

Brand & Patterns

Color & No. Warranty Period

Type of Backing Pad Type

Cost/Unit $ No. of Units Total $

Installed by Date Cost

Cleaned/Refinished by

Date 1 Cost

Date 2 Cost

Date 3 Cost

Ceiling Covering

Type of Covering

Purchased from Date

Brand & Pattern

Color & No. Warranty Period

Applied with

Cost/Unit $ No. of Units Total $

Installed by Date Cost

Notes

Window Covering

Window 1

Measurements

Height   Width

Top of Window to Floor   Trim Width

Type of Covering

Purchased from   Cost   Date

Measurements of Window Covering

Material & Cleaning Instructions

Cleaned by   Cost   Date

Cleaned by   Cost   Date

Window 2

Measurements

Height   Width

Top of Window to Floor   Trim Width

Type of Covering

Purchased from   Cost   Date

Measurements of Window Covering

Material & Cleaning Instructions

Cleaned by   Cost   Date

Cleaned by   Cost   Date

Window 3

Measurements

Height   Width

Top of Window to Floor   Trim Width

Type of Covering

Purchased from   Cost   Date

Measurements of Window Covering

Material & Cleaning Instructions

Cleaned by   Cost   Date

Cleaned by   Cost   Date

Wall Covering

Wall Measurements

North   South   East   West

Use "2nd Type of Covering" for woodwork or paneling. It has a "Refinished by" section.

1st Type of Covering

Purchased from   Date

Brand & Pattern

Color & No.   Warranty Period

Cost/Unit $ No. of Units   Total $

Installed by   Date   Cost

2nd Type of Covering

Purchased from   Date

Brand & Pattern

Color & No.   Warranty Period

Cost/Unit $ No. of Units   Total $

Installed by   Date   Cost

Refinished by   Date   Cost

Doors/Trim

Purchased from	Date
Brand & Style	Material
Stain/Paint Color & No.	Finished with
Installed by	Total Cost
Refinished by	Refinished with
Date	Cost
Hardware Description	
Purchased from	Date
Cost/Unit $ No. of Units	Total $

Furniture/Fixtures

Item	Purchased from	Date	Cost	Warranty

Bedroom Number 4

Floor Covering

Floor Measurements

Widest part of room from middle of doorway

Longest part of room from middle of doorway

Type of Floor

Purchased from   Date

Brand & Patterns

Color & No.   Warranty Period

Type of Backing   Pad Type

Cost/Unit $ No. of Units   Total $

Installed by   Date   Cost

Cleaned/Refinished by

Date 1   Cost

Date 2   Cost

Date 3   Cost

Ceiling Covering

Type of Covering

Purchased from   Date

Brand & Pattern

Color & No.   Warranty Period

Applied with

Cost/Unit $ No. of Units   Total $

Installed by   Date   Cost

Window Covering

Window 1

Measurements

Height	Width
Top of Window to Floor	Trim Width

Type of Covering

Purchased from	Cost	Date

Measurements of Window Covering

Material & Cleaning Instructions

Cleaned by	Cost	Date
Cleaned by	Cost	Date

Window 2

Measurements

Height	Width
Top of Window to Floor	Trim Width

Type of Covering

Purchased from	Cost	Date

Measurements of Window Covering

Material & Cleaning Instructions

Cleaned by	Cost	Date
Cleaned by	Cost	Date

Window 3

Measurements

Height	Width
Top of Window to Floor	Trim Width

Type of Covering

Purchased from   Cost   Date

Measurements of Window Covering

Material & Cleaning Instructions

Cleaned by   Cost   Date

Cleaned by   Cost   Date

Wall Covering

Wall Measurements

North   South   East   West

Use "2nd Type of Covering" for woodwork or paneling. It has a "Refinished by" section.

1st Type of Covering

Purchased from   Date

Brand & Pattern

Color & No.   Warranty Period

Cost/Unit $ No. of Units   Total $

Installed by   Date   Cost

2nd Type of Covering

Purchased from   Date

Brand & Pattern

Color & No.   Warranty Period

Cost/Unit $ No. of Units   Total $

Installed by   Date   Cost

Refinished by   Date   Cost

Doors/Trim

Purchased from	Date
Brand & Style	Material
Stain/Paint Color & No.	Finished with
Installed by	Total Cost
Refinished by	Refinished with
Date	Cost

Hardware Description

Purchased from	Date

Cost/Unit $ No. of Units   Total $

Furniture/Fixtures

Item	Purchased from	Date	Cost	Warranty

Bathroom Number 1

Floor Covering

Floor Measurements

Widest part of room from middle of doorway

Longest part of room from middle of doorway

Type of Floor

Purchased from   Date

Brand & Pattern

Color & No.   Warranty Period

Type of Backing   Pad Type

Cost/Unit $ No. of Units   Total $

Installed by   Attached with

Date   Cost

Cleaned/Refinished by

Date 1   Cost

Date 2   Cost

Date 3   Cost

Ceiling Covering

Type of Covering

Purchased from   Date

Brand & Pattern

Color & No.   Warranty Period

Applied with

Cost/Unit $ No. of Units   Total $

Installed by   Date   Cost

Window Covering

Window 1

Measurements

Height   Width

Top of Window to Floor   Trim Width

Type of Covering

Purchased from   Cost   Date

Measurements of Window Covering

Material & Cleaning Instructions

Cleaned by   Cost   Date

Cleaned by   Cost   Date

Window 2

Measurements

Height   Width

Top of Window to Floor   Trim Width

Type of Covering

Purchased from   Cost   Date

Measurements of Window Covering

Material & Cleaning Instructions

Cleaned by   Cost   Date

Cleaned by   Cost   Date

Wall Covering

Wall Measurements

North   South   East   West

Use "2nd Type of Covering" for woodwork or paneling. It has a "Refinished by" section.

1st Type of Covering

Purchased from   Date

Brand & Pattern

Color & No.   Warranty Period

Cost/Unit $ No. of Units   Total $

Installed by

Date   Cost

2nd Type of Covering

Purchased from   Date

Brand & Pattern

Color & No.   Warranty Period

Cost/Unit $ No. of Units   Total $

Installed by   Date   Cost

Refinished by   Date   Cost

Furniture/Fixtures

Item	Purchased from	Date	Cost	Warranty

Notes

Bathroom Number 2

Floor Covering

Floor Measurements

Widest part of room from middle of doorway

Longest part of room from middle of doorway

Type of Floor

Purchased from   Date

Brand & Pattern

Color & No.   Warranty Period

Type of Backing   Pad Type

Cost/Unit $ No. of Units   Total $

Installed by   Attached with

Date   Cost

Cleaned/Refinished by

Date 1   Cost

Date 2   Cost

Date 3   Cost

Ceiling Covering

Type of Covering

Purchased from   Date

Brand & Pattern

Color & No.   Warranty Period

Applied with

Cost/Unit $ No. of Units   Total $

Installed by   Date   Cost

47

Window Covering

Window 1

Measurements

Height	Width

Top of Window to Floor	Trim Width

Type of Covering

Purchased from	Cost	Date

Measurements of Window Covering

Material & Cleaning Instructions

Cleaned by	Cost	Date

Cleaned by	Cost	Date

Window 2

Measurements

Height	Width

Top of Window to Floor	Trim Width

Type of Covering

Purchased from	Cost	Date

Measurements of Window Covering

Material & Cleaning Instructions

Cleaned by	Cost	Date

Cleaned by	Cost	Date

Wall Covering

Wall Measurements

North	South	East	West

Use "2nd Type of Covering" for woodwork or paneling. It has a "Refinished by" section.

1st Type of Covering

Purchased from	Date
Brand & Pattern	
Color & No.	Warranty Period
Cost/Unit $	No. of Units	Total $
Installed by	
Date	Cost

2nd Type of Covering

Purchased from	Date
Brand & Pattern	
Color & No.	Warranty Period
Cost/Unit $	No. of Units	Total $
Installed by	Date	Cost
Refinished by	Date	Cost

Furniture/Fixtures

Item	Purchased from	Date	Cost	Warranty

Bathroom Number 3

Floor Covering

Floor Measurements

Widest part of room from middle of doorway

Longest part of room from middle of doorway

Type of Floor

Purchased from   Date

Brand & Pattern

Color & No.   Warranty Period

Type of Backing   Pad Type

Cost/Unit $ No. of Units   Total $

Installed by   Attached with

Date   Cost

Cleaned/Refinished by

Date 1   Cost

Date 2   Cost

Date 3   Cost

Ceiling Covering

Type of Covering

Purchased from   Date

Brand & Pattern

Color & No.   Warranty Period

Applied with

Cost/Unit $ No. of Units   Total $

Installed by   Date   Cost

Window Covering

Window 1

Measurements

Height _____ Width _____

Top of Window to Floor _____ Trim Width _____

Type of Covering

Purchased from _____ Cost _____ Date _____

Measurements of Window Covering

Material & Cleaning Instructions _____

Cleaned by _____ Cost _____ Date _____

Cleaned by _____ Cost _____ Date _____

Window 2

Measurements

Height _____ Width _____

Top of Window to Floor _____ Trim Width _____

Type of Covering

Purchased from _____ Cost _____ Date _____

Measurements of Window Covering

Material & Cleaning Instructions _____

Cleaned by _____ Cost _____ Date _____

Cleaned by _____ Cost _____ Date _____

Wall Covering

Wall Measurements

North _____ South _____ East _____ West _____

Use "2nd Type of Covering" for woodwork or paneling. It has a "Refinished by" section.

1st Type of Covering

Purchased from   Date

Brand & Pattern

Color & No.   Warranty Period

Cost/Unit $ No. of Units   Total $

Installed by

Date   Cost

2nd Type of Covering

Purchased from   Date

Brand & Pattern

Color & No.   Warranty Period

Cost/Unit $ No. of Units   Total $

Installed by   Date   Cost

Refinished by   Date   Cost

Furniture/Fixtures

Item	Purchased from	Date	Cost	Warranty

Notes

Den/Study/Office

Floor Covering

Floor Measurements

Widest part of room from middle of doorway

Longest part of room from middle of doorway

Type of Floor

Purchased from   Date

Brand & Patterns

Color & No.   Warranty Period

Type of Backing   Pad Type

Cost/Unit $ No. of Units   Total $

Installed by   Date   Cost

Cleaned/Refinished by

Date 1   Cost

Date 2   Cost

Date 3   Cost

Ceiling Covering

Type of Covering

Purchased from   Date

Brand & Pattern

Color & No.   Warranty Period

Applied with

Cost/Unit $ No. of Units   Total $

Installed by   Date   Cost

Window Covering

Window 1

Measurements

Height   Width

Top of Window to Floor   Trim Width

Type of Covering

Purchased from   Cost   Date

Measurements of Window Covering

Material & Cleaning Instructions

Cleaned by   Cost   Date

Cleaned by   Cost   Date

Window 2

Measurements

Height   Width

Top of Window to Floor   Trim Width

Type of Covering

Purchased from   Cost   Date

Measurements of Window Covering

Material & Cleaning Instructions

Cleaned by   Cost   Date

Cleaned by   Cost   Date

Window 3

Measurements

Height   Width

Top of Window to Floor   Trim Width

Type of Covering

Purchased from	Cost	Date

Measurements of Window Covering

Material & Cleaning Instructions

Cleaned by	Cost	Date
Cleaned by	Cost	Date

Wall Covering

Wall Measurements

North	South	East	West

Use "2nd Type of Covering" for woodwork or paneling. It has a "Refinished by" section.

1st Type of Covering

Purchased from	Date
Brand & Pattern	
Color & No.	Warranty Period

Cost/Unit $	No. of Units	Total $

Installed by	Date	Cost

2nd Type of Covering

Purchased from	Date
Brand & Pattern	
Color & No.	Warranty Period

Cost/Unit $	No. of Units	Total $

Installed by	Date	Cost
Refinished by	Date	Cost

Doors/Trim

Purchased from   Date

Brand & Style   Material

Stain/Paint Color & No.   Finished with

Installed by   Total Cost

Refinished by   Refinished with

Date   Cost

Hardware Description

Purchased from   Date

Cost/Unit $ No. of Units   Total $

Furniture/Fixtures

Item	Purchased from	Date	Cost	Warranty

Family Room

Floor Covering

Floor Measurements

Widest part of room from middle of doorway

Longest part of room from middle of doorway

Type of Floor

Purchased from   Date

Brand & Patterns

Color & No.   Warranty Period

Type of Backing   Pad Type

Cost/Unit $ No. of Units   Total $

Installed by   Date   Cost

Cleaned/Refinished by

Date 1   Cost

Date 2   Cost

Date 3   Cost

Ceiling Covering

Type of Covering

Purchased from   Date

Brand & Pattern

Color & No.   Warranty Period

Applied with

Cost/Unit $ No. of Units   Total $

Installed by   Date   Cost

Window Covering

Window 1

Measurements

Height   Width

Top of Window to Floor   Trim Width

Type of Covering

Purchased from   Cost   Date

Measurements of Window Covering

Material & Cleaning Instructions

Cleaned by   Cost   Date

Cleaned by   Cost   Date

Window 2

Measurements

Height   Width

Top of Window to Floor   Trim Width

Type of Covering

Purchased from   Cost   Date

Measurements of Window Covering

Material & Cleaning Instructions

Cleaned by   Cost   Date

Cleaned by   Cost   Date

Window 3

Measurements

Height   Width

Top of Window to Floor   Trim Width

Type of Covering

Purchased from		Cost	Date

Measurements of Window Covering

Material & Cleaning Instructions

Cleaned by		Cost	Date

Cleaned by		Cost	Date

Wall Covering

Wall Measurements

North	South	East	West

Use "2nd Type of Covering" for woodwork or paneling. It has a "Refinished by" section.

1st Type of Covering

Purchased from	Date

Brand & Pattern

Color & No.	Warranty Period

Cost/Unit $	No. of Units	Total $

Installed by	Date	Cost

2nd Type of Covering

Purchased from	Date

Brand & Pattern

Color & No.	Warranty Period

Cost/Unit $	No. of Units	Total $

Installed by	Date	Cost

Refinished by	Date	Cost

Doors/Trim

Purchased from   Date

Brand & Style   Material

Stain/Paint Color & No.   Finished with

Installed by   Total Cost

Refinished by   Refinished with

Date   Cost

Hardware Description

Purchased from   Date

Cost/Unit $ No. of Units   Total $

Furniture/Fixtures

Item	Purchased from	Date	Cost	Warranty

Notes

Hallway/Stairway 1

Floor Covering

Floor Measurements

Widest part of room from middle of doorway

Longest part of room from middle of doorway

Type of Floor

Purchased from   Date

Brand & Patterns

Color & No.   Warranty Period

Type of Backing   Pad Type

Cost/Unit $ No. of Units   Total $

Installed by   Date   Cost

Cleaned/Refinished by

Date 1   Cost

Date 2   Cost

Date 3   Cost

Ceiling Covering

Type of Covering

Purchased from   Date

Brand & Pattern

Color & No.   Warranty Period

Applied with

Cost/Unit $ No. of Units   Total $

Installed by   Date   Cost

Window Covering

Measurements

Height	Width

Top of Window to Floor	Trim Width

Type of Covering

Purchased from	Cost	Date

Measurements of Window Covering

Material & Cleaning Instructions

Cleaned by	Cost	Date

Cleaned by	Cost	Date

Wall Covering

Wall Measurements

North	South	East	West

Use "2nd Type of Covering" for woodwork or paneling. It has a "Refinished by" section.

1st Type of Covering

Purchased from	Date

Brand & Pattern

Color & No.	Warranty Period

Cost/Unit $	No. of Units	Total $

Installed by	Date	Cost

2nd Type of Covering

Purchased from	Date

Brand & Pattern

Color & No.	Warranty Period

Cost/Unit $	No. of Units	Total $

Installed by	Date	Cost

Refinished by	Date	Cost

Doors/Trim

Purchased from	Date

Brand & Style	Material

Stain/Paint Color & No.	Finished with

Installed by	Total Cost

Refinished by	Refinished with

Date	Cost

Hardware Description

Purchased from	Date

Cost/Unit $	No. of Units	Total $

Furniture/Fixtures

Item	Purchased from	Date	Cost	Warranty

Hallway/Stairway 2

Floor Covering

Floor Measurements

Widest part of room from middle of doorway

Longest part of room from middle of doorway

Type of Floor

Purchased from   Date

Brand & Patterns

Color & No.   Warranty Period

Type of Backing   Pad Type

Cost/Unit $ No. of Units   Total $

Installed by   Date   Cost

Cleaned/Refinished by

Date 1   Cost

Date 2   Cost

Date 3   Cost

Ceiling Covering

Type of Covering

Purchased from   Date

Brand & Pattern

Color & No.   Warranty Period

Applied with

Cost/Unit $ No. of Units   Total $

Installed by   Date   Cost

Window Covering

Measurements

Height	Width

Top of Window to Floor	Trim Width

Type of Covering

Purchased from	Cost	Date

Measurements of Window Covering

Material & Cleaning Instructions

Cleaned by	Cost	Date

Cleaned by	Cost	Date

Wall Covering

Wall Measurements

North	South	East	West

Use "2nd Type of Covering" for woodwork or paneling. It has a "Refinished by" section.

1st Type of Covering

Purchased from	Date

Brand & Pattern

Color & No.	Warranty Period

Cost/Unit $	No. of Units	Total $

Installed by	Date	Cost

2nd Type of Covering

Purchased from	Date

Brand & Pattern

Color & No.	Warranty Period

Cost/Unit $	No. of Units	Total $

Installed by		Date	Cost
Refinished by		Date	Cost

Doors/Trim

Purchased from		Date
Brand & Style		Material
Stain/Paint Color & No.		Finished with
Installed by		Total Cost
Refinished by		Refinished with
Date		Cost
Hardware Description		
Purchased from		Date
Cost/Unit $	No. of Units	Total $

Furniture/Fixtures

Item	Purchased from	Date	Cost	Warranty

Hallway/Stairway 3

Floor Covering

Floor Measurements

Widest part of room from middle of doorway

Longest part of room from middle of doorway

Type of Floor

Purchased from   Date

Brand & Patterns

Color & No.   Warranty Period

Type of Backing   Pad Type

Cost/Unit $ No. of Units   Total $

Installed by   Date   Cost

Cleaned/Refinished by

Date 1   Cost

Date 2   Cost

Date 3   Cost

Ceiling Covering

Type of Covering

Purchased from   Date

Brand & Pattern

Color & No.   Warranty Period

Applied with

Cost/Unit $ No. of Units   Total $

Installed by   Date   Cost

Window Covering

Measurements

Height   Width

Top of Window to Floor   Trim Width

Type of Covering

Purchased from   Cost   Date

Measurements of Window Covering

Material & Cleaning Instructions

Cleaned by   Cost   Date

Cleaned by   Cost   Date

Wall Covering

Wall Measurements

North   South   East   West

Use "2nd Type of Covering" for woodwork or paneling. It has a "Refinished by" section.

1st Type of Covering

Purchased from   Date

Brand & Pattern

Color & No.   Warranty Period

Cost/Unit $ No. of Units   Total $

Installed by   Date   Cost

2nd Type of Covering

Purchased from   Date

Brand & Pattern

Color & No.   Warranty Period

Cost/Unit $ No. of Units   Total $

Installed by	Date	Cost
Refinished by	Date	Cost

Doors/Trim

Purchased from	Date
Brand & Style	Material
Stain/Paint Color & No.	Finished with
Installed by	Total Cost
Refinished by	Refinished with
Date	Cost

Hardware Description

Purchased from	Date

Cost/Unit $	No. of Units	Total $

Furniture/Fixtures

Item	Purchased from	Date	Cost	Warranty

Entry/Foyer/Mud Room

Floor Covering

Floor Measurements

Widest part of room from middle of doorway

Longest part of room from middle of doorway

Type of Floor

Purchased from   Date

Brand & Patterns

Color & No.   Warranty Period

Type of Backing   Pad Type

Cost/Unit $ No. of Units   Total $

Installed by   Date   Cost

Cleaned/Refinished by

Date 1   Cost

Date 2   Cost

Date 3   Cost

Ceiling Covering

Type of Covering

Purchased from   Date

Brand & Pattern

Color & No.   Warranty Period

Applied with

Cost/Unit $ No. of Units   Total $

Installed by   Date   Cost

Window Covering

Measurements

Height   Width

Top of Window to Floor   Trim Width

Type of Covering

Purchased from   Cost   Date

Measurements of Window Covering

Material & Cleaning Instructions

Cleaned by   Cost   Date

Cleaned by   Cost   Date

Wall Covering

Wall Measurements

North   South   East   West

Use "2nd Type of Covering" for woodwork or paneling. It has a "Refinished by" section.

1st Type of Covering

Purchased from   Date

Brand & Pattern

Color & No.   Warranty Period

Cost/Unit $ No. of Units   Total $

Installed by   Date   Cost

2nd Type of Covering

Purchased from   Date

Brand & Pattern

Color & No.   Warranty Period

Cost/Unit $ No. of Units   Total $

Installed by	Date	Cost
Refinished by	Date	Cost

Doors/Trim

Purchased from	Date
Brand & Style	Material
Stain/Paint Color & No.	Finished with
Installed by	Total Cost
Refinished by	Refinished with
Date	Cost

Hardware Description

Purchased from	Date

Cost/Unit $	No. of Units	Total $

Furniture/Fixtures

Item	Purchased from	Date	Cost	Warranty

Laundry Room

Floor Covering

Floor Measurements

Widest part of room from middle of doorway

Longest part of room from middle of doorway

Type of Floor

Purchased from   Date

Brand & Patterns

Color & No.   Warranty Period

Type of Backing   Pad Type

Cost/Unit $ No. of Units   Total $

Installed by   Date   Cost

Cleaned/Refinished by

Date 1   Cost

Date 2   Cost

Date 3   Cost

Ceiling Covering

Type of Covering

Purchased from   Date

Brand & Pattern

Color & No.   Warranty Period

Applied with

Cost/Unit $ No. of Units   Total $

Installed by   Date   Cost

Window Covering

Measurements

Height   Width

Top of Window to Floor   Trim Width

Type of Covering

Purchased from   Cost   Date

Measurements of Window Covering

Material & Cleaning Instructions

Cleaned by   Cost   Date

Cleaned by   Cost   Date

Wall Covering

Wall Measurements

North   South   East   West

Use "2nd Type of Covering" for woodwork or paneling. It has a "Refinished by" section.

1st Type of Covering

Purchased from   Date

Brand & Pattern

Color & No.   Warranty Period

Cost/Unit $ No. of Units   Total $

Installed by   Date   Cost

2nd Type of Covering

Purchased from   Date

Brand & Pattern

Color & No.   Warranty Period

Cost/Unit $ No. of Units   Total $

Installed by		Date	Cost

Refinished by		Date	Cost

Doors/Trim

Purchased from	Date

Brand & Style	Material

Stain/Paint Color & No.	Finished with

Installed by	Total Cost

Refinished by	Refinished with

Date	Cost

Hardware Description

Purchased from	Date

Cost/Unit $	No. of Units	Total $

Major Appliances

Type

Manufacturer	Model/Lot No.	Serial No.

Purchased from		Cost	Date

Authorized Service Center

Warranty Period	Maintenance/Service

Type

Manufacturer	Model/Lot No.	Serial No.

Purchased from		Cost	Date

Authorized Service Center

Warranty Period	Maintenance/Service

Type

Manufacturer	Model/Lot No.	Serial No.

Purchased from   Cost   Date

Authorized Service Center

Warranty Period   Maintenance/Service

Type

Manufacturer   Model/Lot No.   Serial No.

Purchased from   Cost   Date

Authorized Service Center

Warranty Period   Maintenance/Service

Furniture/Fixtures

Item	Purchased from	Date	Cost	Warranty

Attic

Floor Covering

Floor Measurements

Widest part of room from middle of doorway

Longest part of room from middle of doorway

Type of Floor

Purchased from   Date

Brand & Patterns

Color & No.   Warranty Period

Type of Backing   Pad Type

Cost/Unit $ No. of Units   Total $

Installed by   Date   Cost

Cleaned/Refinished by

Date 1   Cost

Date 2   Cost

Date 3   Cost

Ceiling Covering

Type of Covering

Purchased from   Date

Brand & Pattern

Color & No.   Warranty Period

Applied with

Cost/Unit $ No. of Units   Total $

Installed by   Date   Cost

Window Covering

Window 1

Measurements

Height   Width

Top of Window to Floor   Trim Width

Type of Covering

Purchased from   Cost   Date

Measurements of Window Covering

Material & Cleaning Instructions

Cleaned by   Cost   Date

Cleaned by   Cost   Date

Window 2

Measurements

Height   Width

Top of Window to Floor   Trim Width

Type of Covering

Purchased from   Cost   Date

Measurements of Window Covering

Material & Cleaning Instructions

Cleaned by   Cost   Date

Cleaned by   Cost   Date

Window 3

Measurements

Height   Width

Top of Window to Floor   Trim Width

Type of Covering

Purchased from		Cost	Date

Measurements of Window Covering

Material & Cleaning Instructions

Cleaned by		Cost	Date
Cleaned by		Cost	Date

Wall Covering

Wall Measurements

North	South	East	West

Use "2nd Type of Covering" for woodwork or paneling. It has a "Refinished by" section.

1st Type of Covering

Purchased from		Date

Brand & Pattern

Color & No.	Warranty Period

Cost/Unit $	No. of Units	Total $

Installed by	Date	Cost

2nd Type of Covering

Purchased from		Date

Brand & Pattern

Color & No.	Warranty Period

Cost/Unit $	No. of Units	Total $

Installed by	Date	Cost

Refinished by	Date	Cost

Doors/Trim

Purchased from   Date

Brand & Style   Material

Stain/Paint Color & No.   Finished with

Installed by   Total Cost

Refinished by   Refinished with

Date   Cost

Hardware Description

Purchased from   Date

Cost/Unit $ No. of Units   Total $

Furniture/Fixtures

Item	Purchased from	Date	Cost	Warranty

Basement

Floor Covering

Floor Measurements

Widest part of room from middle of doorway

Longest part of room from middle of doorway

Type of Floor

Purchased from   Date

Brand & Patterns

Color & No.   Warranty Period

Type of Backing   Pad Type

Cost/Unit $ No. of Units   Total $

Installed by   Date   Cost

Cleaned/Refinished by

Date 1   Cost

Date 2   Cost

Date 3   Cost

Ceiling Covering

Type of Covering

Purchased from   Date

Brand & Pattern

Color & No.   Warranty Period

Applied with

Cost/Unit $ No. of Units   Total $

Installed by   Date   Cost

Window Covering

Window 1

Measurements

Height   Width

Top of Window to Floor   Trim Width

Type of Covering

Purchased from   Cost   Date

Measurements of Window Covering

Material & Cleaning Instructions

Cleaned by   Cost   Date

Cleaned by   Cost   Date

Window 2

Measurements

Height   Width

Top of Window to Floor   Trim Width

Type of Covering

Purchased from   Cost   Date

Measurements of Window Covering

Material & Cleaning Instructions

Cleaned by   Cost   Date

Cleaned by   Cost   Date

Window 3

Measurements

Height   Width

Top of Window to Floor   Trim Width

Type of Covering

Purchased from   Cost   Date

Measurements of Window Covering

Material & Cleaning Instructions

Cleaned by   Cost   Date

Cleaned by   Cost   Date

Wall Covering

Wall Measurements

North   South   East   West

Use "2nd Type of Covering" for woodwork or paneling. It has a "Refinished by" section.

1st Type of Covering

Purchased from   Date

Brand & Pattern

Color & No.   Warranty Period

Cost/Unit $ No. of Units   Total $

Installed by   Date   Cost

2nd Type of Covering

Purchased from   Date

Brand & Pattern

Color & No.   Warranty Period

Cost/Unit $ No. of Units   Total $

Installed by   Date   Cost

Refinished by   Date   Cost

Doors/Trim

Purchased from _____ Date _____

Brand & Style _____ Material _____

Stain/Paint Color & No. _____ Finished with _____

Installed by _____ Total Cost _____

Refinished by _____ Refinished with _____

Date _____ Cost _____

Hardware Description _____

Purchased from _____ Date _____

Cost/Unit $ _____ No. of Units _____ Total $ _____

Furniture/Fixtures

Item	Purchased from	Date	Cost	Warranty

Miscellaneous Room 1

Floor Covering

Floor Measurements

Widest part of room from middle of doorway

Longest part of room from middle of doorway

Type of Floor

Purchased from   Date

Brand & Patterns

Color & No.   Warranty Period

Type of Backing   Pad Type

Cost/Unit $ No. of Units   Total $

Installed by   Date   Cost

Cleaned/Refinished by

Date 1   Cost

Date 2   Cost

Date 3   Cost

Ceiling Covering

Type of Covering

Purchased from   Date

Brand & Pattern

Color & No.   Warranty Period

Applied with

Cost/Unit $ No. of Units   Total $

Installed by   Date   Cost

Window Covering

Window 1

Measurements

Height   Width

Top of Window to Floor   Trim Width

Type of Covering

Purchased from   Cost   Date

Measurements of Window Covering

Material & Cleaning Instructions

Cleaned by   Cost   Date

Cleaned by   Cost   Date

Window 2

Measurements

Height   Width

Top of Window to Floor   Trim Width

Type of Covering

Purchased from   Cost   Date

Measurements of Window Covering

Material & Cleaning Instructions

Cleaned by   Cost   Date

Cleaned by   Cost   Date

Window 3

Measurements

Height   Width

Top of Window to Floor   Trim Width

Type of Covering

Purchased from	Cost	Date

Measurements of Window Covering

Material & Cleaning Instructions

Cleaned by	Cost	Date

Cleaned by	Cost	Date

Wall Covering

Wall Measurements

North	South	East	West

Use "2nd Type of Covering" for woodwork or paneling. It has a "Refinished by" section.

1st Type of Covering

Purchased from	Date

Brand & Pattern

Color & No.	Warranty Period

Cost/Unit $	No. of Units	Total $

Installed by	Date	Cost

2nd Type of Covering

Purchased from	Date

Brand & Pattern

Color & No.	Warranty Period

Cost/Unit $	No. of Units	Total $

Installed by	Date	Cost

Refinished by	Date	Cost

Doors/Trim

Purchased from   Date

Brand & Style   Material

Stain/Paint Color & No.   Finished with

Installed by   Total Cost

Refinished by   Refinished with

Date   Cost

Hardware Description

Purchased from   Date

Cost/Unit $ No. of Units   Total $

Furniture/Fixtures

Item	Purchased from	Date	Cost	Warranty

Miscellaneous Room 2

Floor Covering

Floor Measurements

Widest part of room from middle of doorway

Longest part of room from middle of doorway

Type of Floor

Purchased from   Date

Brand & Patterns

Color & No.   Warranty Period

Type of Backing   Pad Type

Cost/Unit $ No. of Units   Total $

Installed by   Date   Cost

Cleaned/Refinished by

Date 1   Cost

Date 2   Cost

Date 3   Cost

Ceiling Covering

Type of Covering

Purchased from   Date

Brand & Pattern

Color & No.   Warranty Period

Applied with

Cost/Unit $ No. of Units   Total $

Installed by   Date   Cost

Window Covering

Window 1

Measurements

Height   Width

Top of Window to Floor   Trim Width

Type of Covering

Purchased from   Cost   Date

Measurements of Window Covering

Material & Cleaning Instructions

Cleaned by   Cost   Date

Cleaned by   Cost   Date

Window 2

Measurements

Height   Width

Top of Window to Floor   Trim Width

Type of Covering

Purchased from   Cost   Date

Measurements of Window Covering

Material & Cleaning Instructions

Cleaned by   Cost   Date

Cleaned by   Cost   Date

Window 3

Measurements

Height   Width

Top of Window to Floor   Trim Width

Type of Covering

Purchased from	Cost	Date

Measurements of Window Covering

Material & Cleaning Instructions

Cleaned by	Cost	Date

Cleaned by	Cost	Date

Wall Covering

Wall Measurements

North	South	East	West

Use "2nd Type of Covering" for woodwork or paneling. It has a "Refinished by" section.

1st Type of Covering

Purchased from	Date

Brand & Pattern

Color & No.	Warranty Period

Cost/Unit $	No. of Units	Total $

Installed by	Date	Cost

2nd Type of Covering

Purchased from	Date

Brand & Pattern

Color & No.	Warranty Period

Cost/Unit $	No. of Units	Total $

Installed by	Date	Cost

Refinished by	Date	Cost

Doors/Trim

Purchased from   Date

Brand & Style   Material

Stain/Paint Color & No.   Finished with

Installed by   Total Cost

Refinished by   Refinished with

Date   Cost

Hardware Description

Purchased from   Date

Cost/Unit $ No. of Units   Total $

Furniture/Fixtures

Item	Purchased from	Date	Cost	Warranty

Miscellaneous Room 3

Floor Covering

Floor Measurements

Widest part of room from middle of doorway

Longest part of room from middle of doorway

Type of Floor

Purchased from   Date

Brand & Patterns

Color & No.   Warranty Period

Type of Backing   Pad Type

Cost/Unit $ No. of Units   Total $

Installed by   Date   Cost

Cleaned/Refinished by

Date 1   Cost

Date 2   Cost

Date 3   Cost

Ceiling Covering

Type of Covering

Purchased from   Date

Brand & Pattern

Color & No.   Warranty Period

Applied with

Cost/Unit $ No. of Units   Total $

Installed by   Date   Cost

Window Covering

Window 1

Measurements

Height   Width

Top of Window to Floor   Trim Width

Type of Covering

Purchased from   Cost   Date

Measurements of Window Covering

Material & Cleaning Instructions

Cleaned by   Cost   Date

Cleaned by   Cost   Date

Window 2

Measurements

Height   Width

Top of Window to Floor   Trim Width

Type of Covering

Purchased from   Cost   Date

Measurements of Window Covering

Material & Cleaning Instructions

Cleaned by   Cost   Date

Cleaned by   Cost   Date

Window 3

Measurements

Height   Width

Top of Window to Floor		Trim Width	

Type of Covering

Purchased from		Cost	Date

Measurements of Window Covering

Material & Cleaning Instructions			

Cleaned by		Cost	Date

Cleaned by		Cost	Date

Wall Covering

Wall Measurements

North	South	East	West

Use "2nd Type of Covering" for woodwork or paneling. It has a "Refinished by" section.

1st Type of Covering

Purchased from		Date	

Brand & Pattern			

Color & No.		Warranty Period	

Cost/Unit $	No. of Units	Total $	

Installed by		Date	Cost

2nd Type of Covering

Purchased from		Date	

Brand & Pattern			

Color & No.		Warranty Period	

Cost/Unit $	No. of Units	Total $	

Installed by		Date	Cost

Refinished by		Date	Cost

Doors/Trim

Purchased from   Date

Brand & Style   Material

Stain/Paint Color & No.   Finished with

Installed by   Total Cost

Refinished by   Refinished with

Date   Cost

Hardware Description

Purchased from   Date

Cost/Unit $ No. of Units   Total $

Furniture/Fixtures

Item	Purchased from	Date	Cost	Warranty

Notes

Storage/Closets

Samples/Swatches

Attach swatch or paint daub or before & after photos for each room

Living Room

_____

_____

_____

_____

_____

_____

_____

_____

_____

_____

Dining Room

_____

_____

_____

_____

_____

_____

_____

_____

_____

_____

Notes

Kitchen

Bedroom 1

Bedroom 2

Bedroom 3

Notes

Bedroom 4

Bathroom 1

Bathroom 2

Bathroom 3

Den/Study/Office

Family Room

Hallway/Stairway 1

Hallway/Stairway 2

Hallway/Stairway 3

Entry/Foyer/Mud Room

Laundry Room

Attic

Basement

_____

_____

_____

_____

_____

_____

_____

_____

_____

Miscellaneous Room 1

_____

_____

_____

_____

_____

_____

_____

_____

_____

Miscellaneous Room 2

Miscellaneous Room 3

 # Exterior

Deck

Type of Wood

Purchased from   Date

Sealed/Finished with

Misc. Materials

Installed by   Total $

Refinished with   Date

Contractor   Cost

Refinished with   Date

Contractor   Cost

Refinished with   Date

Contractor   Cost

Driveway

Type of Driveway

Installed by

Cost   Date

Sealed with

Purchased from/Contractor   Date

Cost/Unit $ No. of Units   Total $

Sealed with

Purchased from/Contractor   Date

Cost/Unit $ No. of Units   Total $

Sealed with

Purchased from/Contractor   Date

Cost/Unit $	No. of Units	Total $

Sealed with

Purchased from/Contractor		Date

Cost/Unit $	No. of Units	Total $

Fences

1st Fence

Type of Material

Purchased from		Date

Finished with

Installed by

Total $	Date	

Refinished with		Date

Contractor		Cost

Refinished with		Date

Contractor		Cost

2nd Fence

Type of Material

Purchased from		Date

Finished with

Installed by

Total $	Date	

Refinished with		Date

Contractor		Cost

Refinished with		Date

Contractor		Cost

Gazebo

Type of Material

Installed by

Cost   Date

Sealed with

Contractor   Date

Cost/Unit $ No. of Units   Total $

Sealed with

Contractor   Date

Cost/Unit $ No. of Units   Total $

Patio

Type of Material

Installed by

Cost   Date

Sealed with

Contractor   Date

Cost/Unit $ No. of Units   Total $

Sealed with

Contractor   Date

Cost/Unit $ No. of Units   Total $

Porch

Type of Material

Installed by

Cost   Date

Sealed with

Contractor   Date

Cost/Unit $ No. of Units   Total $

Sealed with

Contractor   Date

Cost/Unit $ No. of Units   Total $

Storage Sheds/Out Buildings

1st Building

Type of Material

Installed by

Cost   Date

Sealed with

Contractor   Date

Cost/Unit $ No. of Units   Total $

Sealed with

Contractor   Date

Cost/Unit $ No. of Units   Total $

Installed by

Cost   Date

Sealed with

Contractor   Date

Cost/Unit $ No. of Units   Total $

Sealed with

Contractor   Date

Cost/Unit $ No. of Units   Total $

2nd Building

Type of Material

Installed by

Cost   Date

Sealed with

Contractor   Date

Cost/Unit $ No. of Units   Total $

Sealed with

Contractor   Date

Cost/Unit $ No. of Units   Total $

Installed by

Cost   Date

Sealed with

Contractor   Date

Cost/Unit $ No. of Units   Total $

Sealed with

Contractor   Date

Cost/Unit $ No. of Units   Total $

Garage

Floor

Type of Floor

Installed by

Cost   Date

Sealed/Finished with

Purchased from   Date

Cost/Unit $ No. of Units   Total $

Maintenance

Gutters & Downspouts

Type of Material

Installed by   Warranty Period

Cost   Date

Purchased from   Date

Cost/Unit $ No. of Units   Total $

Roof

Type of Roofing

Purchased from   Date

Brand, Color & No.   Warranty Period

Cost/Unit $ No. of Units   Total $

Misc. Materials   Cost

Installed by   Cost

Total Materials Cost

Entire Job Cost

Maintenance

Siding

1st Type of Siding

Supplier   Date

Brand, Color & No.   Warranty Period

Cost/Unit $ No. of Units   Total $

Type of Finish

Cost/Unit $ No. of Units   Total $

Purchased from   Date

Installed by   Warranty Period

2nd Type of Siding

Supplier   Date

Brand, Color & No.   Warranty Period

Cost/Unit $ No. of Units   Total $

Type of Finish

Cost/Unit $ No. of Units   Total $

Purchased from   Date

Installed by   Warranty Period

3rd Type of Siding

Supplier   Date

Brand, Color & No.   Warranty Period

Cost/Unit $ No. of Units   Total $

Type of Finish

Cost/Unit $ No. of Units   Total $

Purchased from   Date

Installed by   Warranty Period

Notes

Trim

1st Type of Trim

Supplier   Date

Brand, Color & No.   Warranty Period

Cost/Unit $ No. of Units   Total $

Type of Finish

Cost/Unit $ No. of Units   Total $

Purchased from   Date

Installed by   Warranty Period

2nd Type of Trim

Supplier   Date

Brand, Color & No.   Warranty Period

Cost/Unit $ No. of Units   Total $

Type of Finish

Cost/Unit $ No. of Units   Total $

Purchased from   Date

Installed by   Warranty Period

Walls and Ceiling

Type of Material

Purchased from   Date

Sealed/Finished with   Warranty Period

Cost/Unit $ No. of Units   Total $

House Exterior

Gutters & Downspouts

Type of Material

Installed by   Warranty Period

Cost   Date

Purchased from   Date

Cost/Unit $ No. of Units   Total $

Roof

Type of Roofing

Purchased from   Date

Brand, Color & No.   Warranty Period

Cost/Unit $ No. of Units   Total $

Misc. Materials   Cost

Installed by

Cost   Date

Total Materials Cost

Entire Job Cost

Maintenance

Siding

1st Type of Siding

Supplier   Date

Brand, Color & No.   Warranty Period

Cost/Unit $ No. of Units   Total $

Type of Finish

Cost/Unit $ No. of Units   Total $

Purchased from		Date
Installed by		Warranty Period

2nd Type of Siding

Supplier		Date
Brand, Color & No.		Warranty Period
Cost/Unit $	No. of Units	Total $
Type of Finish		
Cost/Unit $	No. of Units	Total $
Purchased from		Date
Installed by		Warranty Period

3rd Type of Siding

Supplier		Date
Brand, Color & No.		Warranty Period
Cost/Unit $	No. of Units	Total $
Type of Finish		
Cost/Unit $	No. of Units	Total $
Purchased from		Date
Installed by		Warranty Period

Storm Doors

1st Type of Door

Supplier		Date
Brand, Color & No.		Warranty Period
Cost/Unit $	No. of Units	Total $
Type of Finish		
Cost/Unit $	No. of Units	Total $

Purchased from   Date

Installed by   Warranty Period

2nd Type of Door

Supplier   Date

Brand, Color & No.   Warranty Period

Cost/Unit $ No. of Units   Total $

Type of Finish

Cost/Unit $ No. of Units   Total $

Purchased from   Date

Installed by   Warranty Period

Storm Windows

1st Type of Frame

(use "Trim" on next page for "Type of Finish")

Purchased from

Date   Warranty Period

Cost/Unit $ No. of Units   Total $

Installed by

Cost   Date

2nd Type of Frame

(use "Trim" on next page for "Type of Finish")

Purchased from

Date   Warranty Period

Cost/Unit $ No. of Units   Total $

Installed by

Cost   Date

Trim

1st Type of Trim

Supplier   Date
_____

Brand, Color & No.   Warranty Period
_____

Cost/Unit $ No. of Units   Total $
_____

Type of Finish
_____

Cost/Unit $ No. of Units   Total $
_____

Purchased from   Date
_____

Installed by   Warranty Period
_____

2nd Type of Trim

Supplier   Date
_____

Brand, Color & No.   Warranty Period
_____

Cost/Unit $ No. of Units   Total $
_____

Type of Finish
_____

Cost/Unit $ No. of Units   Total $
_____

Purchased from   Date
_____

Installed by   Warranty Period
_____

3rd Type of Trim

Supplier   Date
_____

Brand, Color & No.   Warranty Period
_____

Cost/Unit $ No. of Units   Total $
_____

Type of Finish
_____

Cost/Unit $ No. of Units   Total $
_____

Purchased from   Date
_____

Installed by   Warranty Period
_____

🏠 Gardening/Landscaping

Garden Diary/Phenology

1st/Earliest

1st/ Earliest

Last

Last

Most Rain

Heat Wave/ Highest Temp.

Cold Wave/ Coldest Temp.

Last Snow/Most Snow

Record Vegetable Size or Harvest

Bird Sightings

Wildlife Sightings

Other

Trees/Shrubs

Plant Type	Size	Qty.	Cost	Date	Supplier

Special Care/Notes:

Perennials

Plant Type	Size	Qty.	Cost	Date	Supplier

Special Care/Notes:

Vegetable Garden

Plant Type	Size	Qty.	Cost	Date	Supplier

Special Care/Notes:

Garden/Yard Diagram

Notes

Garden/Yard Diagram

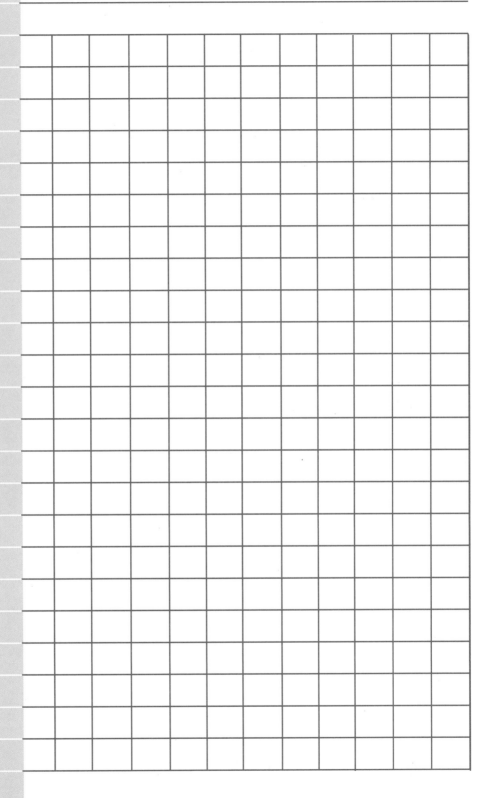

Waterfall/Water Garden/Fountain

Type

Material	Qty.	Cost	Date	Warranty	Supplier

Pump

Size   Cost   Date   Warranty

Installed by

Electrical Lights

Purchased from   Date

Cost   Warranty

Installed by

Cost   Date

126

Notes

Cleaning

Chemical Treatment

Maintenance

Plant Type

Qty.	Cost	Date	Supplier

Fish Type

Qty.	Cost	Date	Supplier

Equipment

Type

Mfr.

Model   Serial No.

Purchased from   Cost

Date   Warranty

Maintenance/Service

Type

Mfr.

Model   Serial No.

Purchased from   Cost

Date   Warranty

Maintenance/Service

Type

Mfr.

Model   Serial No.

Purchased from   Cost

Date   Warranty

Maintenance/Service

Type

Mfr.

Model   Serial No.

Purchased from   Cost

Date   Warranty

Maintenance/Service

Type

Mfr.

Model   Serial No.

Purchased from   Cost

Date   Warranty

Maintenance/Service

Type

Mfr.

Model   Serial No.

Purchased from   Cost

Date   Warranty

Maintenance/Service

Type

Mfr.

Model   Serial No.

Purchased from   Cost

Date   Warranty

Maintenance/Service

Type

Mfr.

Model   Serial No.

Purchased from   Cost

Date   Warranty

Maintenance/Service

Portable Items

Arbor/Trellis/Lattice

_____

_____

_____

Barbecue/Grill

_____

_____

_____

Bird Feeders & Baths/Wildlife Feeders

_____

_____

Compost Bin

_____

_____

Lawn Furniture/Picnic Table

_____

_____

_____

_____

_____

Lawn Swing/Glider

_____

_____

_____

Lighting-Outdoor

Ornaments/Statuary/Flower Boxes

Retaining Walls

Swing & Play Sets/Sand Box

Wheelbarrows/Carts/Planting Tables

Yard Tools/Equipment

Lawn/Garden Irrigation & Service

Garden Irrigation

_____

_____

_____

Lawn Maintenance/Service

_____

_____

_____

_____

Sprinkler System

_____

_____

_____

_____

Watering Schedule

_____

_____

_____

_____

_____

_____

_____

Garden/Yard Miscellaneous

Buried Cable/Pipeline Locations

Edging

Mulch

Pests

Soil Samples

Weed Barrier

🏠 Infrastructure

Electrical/Wiring

Cooling & Heating

Air Conditioner

Type of Unit

Manufacturer & Model

Efficiency

Purchased from/Contractor

Date	Cost	Warranty Period

Filter Type	Size

Cleaned/Serviced by

Date No. 1	Cost

Date No. 2	Cost

Date No. 3	Cost

Date No. 4	Cost

Fireplace

Insert Mfr. & Model

Purchased from

Date	Cost	Warranty Period

Installed by

Cost	Date

Chimney Cleaned by

Date No. 1	Cost

Date No. 2	Cost

Date No. 3	Cost

Heat Exchanger

Manufacturer & Model

Efficiency

Purchased from

Date	Cost	Warranty Period

Installed by

Cost	Date

Cleaned/Serviced by

Date No. 1	Cost

Date No. 2	Cost

Date No. 3	Cost

Date No. 4	Cost

Heat Pump

Type of Unit

Manufacturer & Model

Efficiency

Purchased from/Contractor

Date	Cost	Warranty Period

Filter Type	Size

Cleaned/Serviced by

Date No. 1	Cost

Date No. 2	Cost

Date No. 3	Cost

Date No. 4	Cost

Heating Plant (Furnace)

Type of Unit

Manufacturer & Model

Efficiency

Purchased from/Contractor

Date	Cost	Warranty Period

Filter Type   Size

Humidifier

Cleaned/Serviced by

Date No. 1	Cost

Date No. 2	Cost

Date No. 3	Cost

Date No. 4	Cost

Wood Stove

Manufacturer & Model

Efficiency

Purchased from/Contractor

Date	Cost	Warranty Period

Chimney Cleaned by

Date No. 1	Cost

Date No. 2	Cost

Date No. 3	Cost

Date No. 4	Cost

Insulation

Attic

Type of Insulation   Thickness

R-Value Added   Cost

Previous R-Value   Aggregate R-Value

Type of Vapor Barrier (6 mill poly, etc.)

Installed by   Total Material Cost

Labor $ Total $

Type of Venting

Note: You should have one square foot of free-flowing cross-ventilation for every 150 square feet of attic floor space. Soffit vents with screen covers can reduce air flow by up to 75%.

Under Eave (Soffit) Sq.In./Cm

Turbines Sq. In./Cm

Other

Walls

1st Type of Insulation

Thickness   R-Value Added   Cost

2nd Type of Insulation

Thickness   R-Value Added   Cost

Previous R-Value   Aggregate R-Value

Type of Vapor Barrier (6 mill poly, etc.)

Installed by   Total Material Cost

Labor $ Total $

Other Insulation *(rim joist, exterior foundation, etc.)*

Thermostats

Radon Testing & Information

Sewer/Cesspool/Septic System

Sump Pump

Water Heaters

Water Softener

Well

🏠 Miscellaneous

Door Chimes

Garage Door Openers

Intercom System

Security System

Smoke/Fire Detectors

Computer/Printer

Telephones/Answering Machine/Fax

Swimming Pool

Whirlpool/Hot Tub/Sauna

Whole House Vacuum

♠ Calendar

January

☐ Clean out/organize your desk and papers.

☐ Use a humidifier indoors.

☐ Test your security system.

☐ Check roof and gutters for water leaks and ice accumulation.

☐ Beware of uneven snow piles.

☐ Avoid stacking wood where snow will buildup and soak the wood.

☐ Make sure snow and ice equipment i.e. shovels, plows, salt are ready to go.

☐ Remove excess snow from your mailbox, shrubs, and foundation plants.

☐ Know the freeze-thaw cycle for your climate.

February

■ If you have a woodstove, clean it.

■ Keep an eye on humidity levels.

■ Check heating and water pumps.

■ Clean up lent and dust outside the clothes dryer vent.

■ Install more lighting in your darkest corners, inside and outside.

■ Survey driveway, yard, steps, walkways, and garden for faults.

■ Clean floors.

■ Check your water and water main.

March

- [ ] Examine metal railings for deterioration.

- [ ] Look for mold/fungi on wood shingles and roof shakes.

- [ ] Inspect the masonry or cladding and the foundation for weather damage.

- [ ] Look at built-in planters.

- [ ] Test your outdoor outlets.

- [ ] Check for dry rot.

- [ ] Clean, oil, and repair tools and lawn equipment.

- [ ] Measure the air in the tires of your mower and wheelbarrows.

- [ ] Schedule yard and garden services.

- [ ] Examine wood fences and stone walls for cracks, holes, and other problems.

- [ ] Remove excess snow from your mailbox, shrubs, and foundation plants.

- [ ] Take care of gravel, sand, and salt deposited during snow plowing.

April

☐ Wash your windows, inside and out.

☐ Change the batteries in your smoke detectors.

☐ Survey your roof, from your roof.

☐ Check exterior wiring.

☐ Examine windows for rot, cracked panes.

☐ Switch out storm windows with screens.

☐ Check deck, patio, and/or porch for winter weather effects, especially near

garden beds and planters.

☐ Spring clean all surfaces, in and outdoors.

☐ Sweep the garage.

☐ Reinstall your garden hoses.

☐ Check sprinklers and water spouts.

☐ Look for winter damage on retaining walls.

May

■ Check that major appliances are sitting level.

■ Repair lawn areas, and trim winter damaged trees and shrubs.

■ Deodorize/clean carpets and rugs.

■ Switch out your humidifier with a dehumidifier and don't forget the garage.

■ Clean and air-out the basement and attic and also look for leaks.

■ Put in window-unit air conditioners.

■ Get ready to paint exterior surfaces.

■ Set up porch and patio planters.

■ Check outdoor lighting.

■ Prep your swimming pool.

■ Don't forget to look at the pool surround.

■ Repaint and repair trellises.

June

- Exterminate rodents and bugs, inside and out.

- Check for leaky faucets and pipes.

- Change your furnace filter.

- Clear out gutters.

- Wash the exterior walls of your home and garage.

- Examine caulking.

- Don't forget to water and fertilize plants and planters at least twice a week.

- Clean outdoor furniture once a week to once every other week.

- Oil and sharpen all tools and equipment.

- Clean your swimming pool.

- Mow grass once a week or every 10 days.

July

- Look for molds, mildew, and moss inside, outside, and on the roof.

- Run your dehumidifier(s).

- Keep all damp areas clean.

- Keep up gutters and leaders.

- Cool down paved surfaces.

- To keep the number of bugs down, use porch lights sparingly.

- Make sure garage doors are storm-proofed.

- For your lawn: water, water, water.

- Prune maples, birches, lindens, and horse chestnuts.

Notes

August

▦ Test ceiling fans.

▦ Keep cleaning your dehumidifier.

▦ Clean window balances.

▦ Now's the time for any exterior paint touch ups.

▦ Continue to care for outdoor furniture.

▦ Clean and replace garbage cans.

▦ Every week water the lawn.

September

■ Make sure your woodstove is ready to go.

■ Examine your heating system.

■ Survey your radiators.

■ Check chimney flues.

■ Inspect fireplace dampers.

■ Build a stockpile of firewood.

■ Inspect your chimney, including your chimney cap.

■ Look for and seal any rodent entry points.

■ Air out your grass.

■ Continue to mow.

■ If applicable, deer proof.

October

■ Change the batteries in your smoke detectors.

■ Check windows and window frames for condensation, leaks, and repairs

■ Put away your window unit air conditioners.

■ Shut off outdoor faucet valves, put away garden hoses, and turn off automatic sprinklers.

■ Switch out dehumidifier with humidifier.

■ Switch out screens for storm windows.

■ Put away garden hoses.

■ Clean out planters.

■ Store outdoor furniture, yard equipment, and garden tools.

■ Prepare snowblower and other snow equipment.

■ Rake and/or blow leaves.

■ Prepare burlap to protect shrubs.

November

- Inspect vents.

- Make sure heat and hot-water thermostats are set to be energy efficient.

- Clear out gutters, downspouts, and roof valleys of fallen leaves.

- Examine fuel tank for problems, including that it is clear of water.

- Check supports, railings, and stairs.

- Replace broken and burned out light fixtures.

- Clear out space for drainage around garage entrances.

- And check for clogged drainage ditches.

- Keep frequently used areas clear of snow and leaves.

- Use driveway markers to protect your lawn and garden beds.

- Cut your lawn one last time.

December

- Beware of frozen pipes.

- Don't let locks freeze.

- Minimize condensation on window glass.

- Think about adding more insulation.

- Clean out your humidifier.

- Air out your attic and basement.

- Look out for ice everywhere.

- Double-check that you shut off and drained hose bibs.

- Shovel excess snow off walkways, driveways, porches, decks, patios, and garage doors.

- Clean garage door.

- Survey your gardens one last time.

Extra Notes

Notes

Notes

Extra Notes

Extra Notes

Notes

Notes

Extra Notes

Extra Notes

Notes

Extra Notes

Extra Notes